To C

Wi:

Happy & Sucessful
1995.

CW00656323

a BOOK *of* your Own

First published by Quartet Books Limited 1994
A member of the Namara Group
27 Goodge Street
London W1P 1FD

A catalogue record for this title is available
from the British Library

ISBN 0 7043 7079 4
Printed and bound in Great Britain

a BOOK of your Own

Anne DICKSON

Illustrated by Geraldine Bracey

QUARTET ☙ BOOKS

Other titles by Anne Dickson
A Woman In Your Own Right
The Mirror Within

By Anne Dickson and Nikki Henriques
Menopause
Hysterectomy

1 The resolve to be a
different and better person
will soon evaporate;
acceptance of yourself,
as you are, is slower to cultivate
but more steadfast.

It is curious
how often we make the mistake
of using our own behaviour as a
central reference point when
interpreting
other people's
behaviour. 2

3 Really good friends
are those who interrupt
your usual pattern
with a reminder to be
gentle on yourself and
take the easier option.

People are usually quite happy
to consider a clearly expressed request
– it is the accumulated
backlog of resentment
that gets their backs up. 4

5 You can still behave agreeably
without having to
pretend to agree.

When a woman friend or colleague
tries to be assertive
and makes a mess of it,
that is the moment
she needs your support
and congratulations for
having taken the risk. 6

7 Pleasure and pride
are
incompatible
with
anxiety.

Taking the initiative
instead of waiting for someone else
to make the first move,
can be a seriously
liberating experience. 8

9 Learn to distinguish
between
what you can change
and what you can't.

10 Dependence on approval
is like any other addiction
– habit-forming
and desperately
hard to overcome.

11 If you focus only
on the absence of perfection,
you can lose sight of the love
contained in the present.

12 Regular periods of time
for you to experience yourself alone
are as vital
to your emotional health
as sleep.

13 Genuine acknowledgement
of someone's anger
can help defuse
an explosive situation.

Our abiding need to please **14**
robs us of our personal power.

15

Care, given willingly,
is free of charge;
care, given grudgingly,
stores up hidden costs.

Fear of success inhibits us
more powerfully
than fear of failure.

16

17
Rather than
getting lost
in 'what ifs' and 'if onlys',
decide what you will settle for right now
– and go for it.

Half-hearted or grudging participation
in any sexual activity
always stores up
a measure of resentment. **18**

19

Even the very young
and the very old
have the right to
be considered as equals.

Imagine
how you would look upon yourself
if you had always been told
that you were beautiful
– then, for a day,
behave 'as if'.

20

21

Be less mistrustful
of your heart
and more sceptical
of the dictates
of your head.

We try to be in control
so much of the time
that it is hard to allow others
the freedom to have bad moods
without feeling
personally
responsible.

22

23

However secretly
you disapprove of someone,
it will inevitably leak out
in your communication with them.

Setting limits
allows you to value
your time and energy
more highly.

24

25 If you want to trust
something precious
to someone else's care,
you will be extremely careful
who that person is: remember this
when committing yourself to a lover.

Irritation at others' failure
to live up to our expectations
is less destructive
than the pitiless way
we punish ourselves when we
fail to live up to our own. **26**

27

A refusal
with an open heart
allows you to care
and to say no
at the same time.

When the whole situation
makes you unhappy and confused,
choose *one* thing,
however small,
that you would like to change.

28

29

When you look in the mirror
first thing in the morning,
interrupt the critical voices
in your head by looking at
your reflection and saying,
"Good morning, friend."

Criticising others for being too dependent
voices, indirectly,
a desperate longing
to be taken care of ourselves.

30

31

Finding your own voice
is crucial
– learn to breathe deeply,
play with different sounds
and don't worry
about who might hear
or what they might think.

1 Resentment that your needs have been ignored usually indicates that you have confined yourself to wishing, instead of expressing your needs to others.

It is extremely frustrating for others when we persistently avoid taking responsibility for making our own decisions. 2

3 If you wait
until you *feel* assertive
before you tackle
a particular situation,
you'll probably never do it.

Only robots can say no
without feeling guilty. 4

5 Never allow yourself
to be pressurised into making
an instant decision
— always give yourself permission
to ask for time to think it over,
whether you need
an hour, a day or a week.

If we have no clear boundaries,
we can experience
no real freedom. 6

7 It is far easier
to find fault
than give voice
to appreciation.

8 Try to take responsibility
for your refusal
instead of portraying yourself
as a helpless victim of
other people or events.

9 It is assertive to know
when to yield graciously
to impossible odds.

True humility
is only possible
when your self-esteem is high. 10

11

It is never too late in life
to awaken
a dormant talent.

Remember
you are still precious
even when someone treats you
like shit!

12

13 For most of us,
put-downs are
more effectively handled
with honesty and clarity than
with an attempt at wit.

Only conditional love is blind
— true love allows us **14**
to see and love
everything inclusively.

15
The feeling of envy
can offer a lesson
as to where and how
to set your own sights higher.

We often undermine our authority
by indulging our need to be liked
when it would be sufficient
and more appropriate to
settle for being respected.
16

17

The more
you try to change someone,
the more
they will resist.

18

A life spent
constantly restrained by
the need for others' approval
is a life spent
in captivity.

19

It is the holding back
of tears that is painful
– not the release.

However hard we try
to control everything that's happening,
we *still*
get taken
by surprise.

20

21

Your own insight
in your own time
has the greatest
meaning and value.

One way we can put ourselves down
is by failing to ask
for adequate financial
compensation
for the work we do.

22

23 Try and acknowledge
your tiredness
before you collapse
– the longer you leave it,
the harder it becomes to say 'enough'.

If taking your time is what suits you,
assert your right to do so,
even though
this speed-crazy culture **24**
will label you *slow*.

25 The pressure always to be
pleasing in our behaviour
and our appearance
distorts our spirits
in the same way that
the ancient practice
of foot binding
distorted women's feet.

If it *really* didn't matter,
you wouldn't be spending
so much time thinking about it. 26

27 Love and anger are said to be incompatible bedfellows — but they certainly enjoy a passionate and lifelong love affair.

It is important to keep sight of your own beauty even when others fail to see it. **28**

29

Sometimes
the only way
to leap
is to close
your eyes,
surrender
and
trust.

1

It's easy to get trapped
between two narrow alternatives:
either I'm to blame
or you're to blame.
In fact, some things just *happen*.

In reality,
we are rarely held captive
by the demands of others
— more often we are
held captive only by the
limits of our imagination.

2

3 Is it *really* too late?

Take the risk of asking
for a hug
when you feel in need of one. 4

5 Automatic apologies,
however abject,
are usually intended
to deflect the other person's anger:
they have little to do with
genuine assumption of responsibility
or sincere regret.

Just because you're in a minority of one
doesn't necessarily mean
that you are 6
wrong.

7 Making decisions inappropriately
on behalf of others
is a form of oppression.

I am worth respecting
even when
I don't get the respect
I deserve. 8

9 When you ask for more money
it is more effective
to state
the desired sum specifically
than to suggest some vague increase.

Fear of isolation prevents me
from being truly in touch
with my personal power. 10

————— March —————

11
A spontaneous
expression of gratitude
is more valuable than a
planned and polished performance.

It is seductive
but ultimately a waste of energy
to try and bring about
certainty
where there can be none. **12**

13 The longer you wait
to make a move,
the greater your anxiety.

Try simply enjoying our differences
– without the automatic labels
of better
or worse. **14**

15 No-one could make
you *feel* insignificant if
you weren't disposed
to believe
you were insignificant in the first place.

You don't have to
strive to prove
to others you are lovable
– you are lovable
just as you are. **16**

17 Sing, dance, paint
for the sheer pleasure of it
— instead of getting lost in
achieving marks for artistic performance!

An aggressive approach
provokes
an aggressive response. **18**

19 Determination to have everything *now* can prevent us discovering all sorts of other options that lie in store for us if we can only take a deep breath... and wait!

If listening to a particular conversation is making you feel uncomfortable, you can choose to walk away from it. **20**

21
It may only be a tiny grievance, but air it anyway.

22
Value those friends who help you laugh at yourself when you tend to become over-serious.

23 Opening your heart
to the experience of love
inevitably leaves your
heart open to the experience of loss.

Nobody
welcomes criticism. 24

25 Asking clearly
and specifically
lets the other person
know *what* it is you want
– this gives them
a clear choice about
how to respond.

A statement which begins with
'I feel that ...'
is nothing to do
with your feelings
– it is usually a substitute
for "I think ..." **26**

27 If you keep waiting for
the right moment
to speak up you'll find
the moment has passed you by.

Playing the role of 'the martyr'
in the present
encourages the desire
for rescue and reward
in the future. **28**

29

You can enjoy
sexual attraction to someone
without
feeling compelled to *do* anything about it.

The first step
in learning to express your emotions
is to stop lying to yourself
about what
you really feel.

30

31 A little
outrageousness
never did anyone any harm.

1 Simply because a clever put-down
makes others laugh,
it doesn't stop it
being hurtful to the recipient.

Confronting a situation
when it slightly irritates you,
helps you handle it
effectively and harmlessly.
The longer you let the pressure
build up, the more likely you are
to explode with damaging
and hurtful consequences. 2

—————— April ——————

3 Most women find fatigue
very difficult to acknowledge,
so instead of
listening to our bodies,
we often push them
beyond healthy limits.

Instead of fretting
about someone's opinion of you,
channel your energy
into a different approach: 4
ask them directly.

5

Isn't it extraordinary how easily
we hand over
our power
on a plate
and then get so angry when
someone helps themselves to it?

Your sexuality
is a vital part
of your being
even if
you're not currently sexually
'doing' anything.

6

7 Try not to
turn down authentic care,
when offered to you,
even if it isn't packaged
in exactly the way you had in mind.

If you begin by saying,
'Hello, I'm sorry... ',
you introduce yourself
as an apology: you'll
find it hard going trying 8
to move from that starting point.

9 Even good advice,
if excessive,
will obstruct the capacity
of the individual
to think and decide for herself.

Accompanying your refusal
with an explanation can be courteous.
Offering elaborate excuses
is usually an attempt
to persuade the other person
not to disapprove of you. 10

11 If you try to soothe away
someone else's anger
to lessen
your own discomfort,
you'll only make them
angrier.

Remember
when you're down and tired,
you're more likely to interpret
every 'mishap' too personally. **12**

13 If you make
a vague, indifferent request,
you are likely to get
a vague, indifferent response.

It is always tempting
to win
– the price is
loss of equality. 14

——————— April ———————

15 Remind yourself you exist
as *you*,
apart from
all your roles and responsibilities.

Does it really matter
if people think
you're crazy
some of the time? **16**

————— April —————

17 You can approach your life as a unique work of art or as an inherited template which you have to adhere to relentlessly.

Each time you say yes when you really want to say no, you mark up another notch of resentment. **18**

19

Whatever fee you ask for
will be too much
in some people's eyes
and too little in others'.

You don't have to stay and listen
to someone who is talking at you
— you can close
the conversation
and leave.

20

21 If you are certain
of your *right* to a service
you are paying for,
you will be able to complain clearly,
but without putting anyone down.

When making a list of things to do,
add at least one pleasurable activity
for yourself
so that the importance
of taking care of yourself
doesn't entirely
escape your notice. **22**

23 Someone in great distress
sometimes just needs
a caring and quiet presence
— not analysis or advice.

No risk, no change
is ever too small
to be significant. **24**

25

It's easier to stay with the
delusions we've created
in our heads
about others than to discuss matters
openly with them and
experience the shock of
reality.

Care rooted in compassion
is quite different from
care rooted in compulsion:
the former is given willingly,
the latter,
extracted through
fear of censure or disapproval.

26

27 We cannot
be held responsible for
what we feel
— only for how we choose to act
on our feelings.

You can clearly state
your profound disagreement
with someone else's opinion
and *still* leave them the right
to believe what they want. **28**

——————— April ———————

29 It may be
just a little
tiny thing
– but it could well be
an *important* little tiny thing.

In an assertive transaction,
power is an ongoing part of
the process
and has little to do with
who 'wins'. **30**

May

1 The more you can allow others
the freedom to express feelings of
irritation and anger towards you,
the less likely they are
to stockpile resentment.

If a compliment gives you
both embarrassment and pleasure,
it is more rewarding for the other person
if you express both these feelings honestly
than if you
try to disguise your embarrassment
with a hastily contrived compliment
of your own in return. 2

3
Start small
— celebrate
— and build from there.

When we start to assess
the emotional tally of a relationship,
it is an indication that the currency
exchanged in previous transactions
has been guilt
and not
4
freedom of choice.

5 If you say no,
looking at the person directly,
without smiling
and in a firm tone of voice,
they'll know you mean it.

If you are always the one
who gives
in any relationship,
it is you
who retains the power. 6

7 Essentially,
feelings are
neither positive nor negative
– this division is
based on what is
desirable or undesirable
in any given culture.

Each time you acknowledge
your anxiety and go ahead anyway,
you strengthen your self-esteem,
no matter what 8
the outcome.

9 The totally assertive woman
exists only in our minds
— she is not for real!

Both irritation
and pleasure
are best expressed
spontaneously. 10

11 It is difficult to overestimate
the conflict
we face when saying no
because it flies in the face
of all the accommodating behaviour
we have ever learned.

However clear and direct and assertive
a request may *sound*,
it is always aggressive
if it leaves the
other person
with no choice. **12**

13 The lower
our self-esteem,
the greater
our need to be right.

However deeply you're convinced
that you know what is best
for someone else,
you still run the risk of
a subtle,
emotional
take-over. **14**

15

We need to experience
separateness
as much as
we need to experience
closeness.

16

Our endless capacity
for suffering
in the martyr role
is matched only by
our endless capacity
for expecting
adequate compensation.

17 Releasing some of
the stored up feelings
from your past
helps you to be clearer about
what you are feeling
in the present.

However lovingly,
thoughtfully
and caringly,
it is still possible to give people
too much. **18**

19

A steamroller,
no matter how quietly
and gently it moves,
will still crush everything
in its path.

It is hard to allow others
to simply 'forget' things
when we, ourselves, are
trying so hard
to remember everything
for everybody.

20

21 Become familiar
with your emotions
– recognise them,
experience them,
learn not to be frightened of them.

It is easier to accept
someone's disappointment
in the short term
when you know that
your change of mind
is more truthful
for you
in the long term. **22**

23 If your suggestion is ignored,
you can either sulk or
make the suggestion again,
adding clearly that
you would welcome a response.

Learn which elements
soothe and revitalise you
— then make the time to
be near water or fire,
in the air
or close to the earth. 24

25

Although painful,
it is less frightening
to reproach ourselves
for taking wrong decisions than
it is to accept that much of what
happens is beyond our control.

Each time we say, 'I'm no good at…',
we suppress the possibility of
the fun of
learning.

26

27 If you are unable to express intimate feelings of anger and grief with a partner, you will find it difficult to express the vulnerability of sexual arousal.

It is so easy to underestimate the beauty and value of what we give to others. 28

29 It is impossible
to be creative
with your life *and* to worry
about what people think of you
– so the choice is
which one to give up.

Put-downs are powerful
– an unchallenged one
can remain
clear in the memory
for years afterwards. **30**

31

Remind yourself
you're a passionate,
hot-blooded woman
even if no-one currently fancies you.

1 You don't need to understand
why someone's crying
to be supportive
— just *be* there.

When you make a complaint,
include a specific alternative
so that the other person
knows
what you would prefer. 2

3 Our reactions
to others
are rooted in
our own image of ourselves.

Giving
sometimes offers us
an easier, less risky option
than daring to take. 4

5 If, when offering a criticism,
you are aiming for a complete
personality transformation,
you will find your efforts and criticism
understandably rejected.

If you refuse to be strait-jacketed
by other people's expectations,
you'll find
far more creative opportunities 6
open to you.

7 When you've done
the brave and right thing
but are tormented by self-doubt,
contact a loving friend
and ask for reassurance.

As you summon up the courage
to confront a long-standing source
of irritation, take a moment to consider
your own limits — what will you do
if the other person refuses
to agree to change? 8

9 If you find it hard
to confront a put-down,
it may be because
deep down
you are afraid it might be true.

Trying to reach an orgasm in the face of
feeling resentful, tearful or depressed
is a form of
self-denial
and
self-punishment. 10

———————— June ————————

11
Sometimes
the blanket feeling of rejection
is only a thin covering
for a much deeper sense of
outrage.

Don't be afraid
to give a compliment to someone
on the grounds that you
don't know the person
well enough. **12**

— June —

13 Listen attentively
to what your body,
in its wisdom,
tells you.

If you ask for more money at work,
don't be drawn into comparisons with
your colleagues
— keep the discussion
centred on your own request
and your own situation. **14**

15 Trying to make
your father or mother
into the parent
you would have preferred
is a waste of energy.

Taking the time to explore and release
stored-up emotions
can greatly enhance **16**
your self-esteem.

———————————— June ————————————

17 When you catch yourself
thinking, 'If only...',
you'll find
your eyes are closed to the
creative opportunities of the present.

The cloying sweetness
of approval
spoils our taste for
personal power. **18**

19

Suppressing our feelings
of hurt
inevitably
suppresses our feelings
of joy.

If you have something important to say,
always wait until you have
the other person's
full attention
before starting to speak. **20**

21 Learning to rid yourself of a negative self-image is like undoing a Russian doll – you keep thinking you've got to the core of it and then you find there's still another layer.

Pleading powerlessness is sometimes a more comfortable option than acknowledging choice. 22

23 Remember you have
a right to privacy
– don't allow yourself
to be pressurised
into answering questions
which feel intrusive.

Capping one put-down with
another 'better' one
enhances
the use of aggression
as an emotional weapon. 24

25

The problem with
frequently
putting yourself down
is that it makes it difficult
for anyone to get near enough
to offer even
a small honest criticism of their own.

Investing too much effort into
being caring and considerate ourselves
can make us furious with others
who choose not to
live up to our excessively
high standards.

26

27 The more deeply
I reject myself,
the more fearful I become
of being rejected by others.

Go ahead
and be ridiculous! 28

29 However sweetly,
gently or charmingly
you diminish someone,
they will still feel
unmistakably *diminished*.

We often assume that
once a physical wound has healed,
that is the end of it.
We forget
that the emotional wounds
need to be healed as well. 30

1
One way we oppress others
is by denying them
an opportunity
to express their feelings towards us.

Take five minutes
to look into the heart of a flower
— and let your mind be still.
2

3 When you finally get around to
criticising someone's behaviour,
remember that although
you've been aware of your feelings
for months, even years,
they will come as a great surprise
to the other person.

Feeling passionately
puts colour
into a grey world. 4

5 Let yourself
off the hook
– no one else can do it for you.

Next time you are planning a treat
for someone you love,
schedule in 6
a treat for yourself as well.

7

The immense effort
many of us put into controlling
everything and everyone
around us
usually stems from a
deep fear of rejection.

Symptoms of anxiety
are worse when resisted
— if you allow
the sensations in your body
and acknowledge your feeling,
they will pass through and away.

8

9 Once a week,
try a conscious choice to
let go of your need
to be right.

Try to acknowledge
other people's feelings
without judging them. 10

11

Other people's ups and downs
often occur
quite independently
of our efforts
to control their lives for them.

Always take the time to be clear
about what *you* want
before making any move
towards tackling a situation.

12

13

Do you really want
another drink
or are you agreeing
to avoid appearing unsociable?

Personal power
comes from within ourselves
– it is not dependent on
outside approval or status.

14

15

The guilt you feel after saying no is only a measure of how difficult it was for you to do so.

Occasionally allow yourself a break from attending to others' needs – instead of waiting for others to give you their permission and blessing.

16

17
A good cry
can be
a great release.

Aim high
– if you come in low,
you can still praise yourself
highly.
18

19

Vulnerability should never be confused with weakness.

The quality of compassion can easily degenerate into pity and patronage.

20

21

Apportioning blame
too readily
temporarily eases
the insecurity of living with uncertainty.

Our self-esteem is enhanced every time
we face, acknowledge and
survive
any given anxiety.

22

23
If you find yourself
complaining
about always taking
the 'helper' role,
check whether or not you are being
clear about your own needs.

We waste
so much time and energy
striving
to be better than we are. # 24

25 Enjoying your own orgasm
in your own way retrieves
it from being a rateable,
standardised achievement
and returns the experience to
the realms of
personal pleasure.

It is possible to acknowledge our
dependence on others
without losing
our autonomy **26**
or self-respect.

27 Rudeness is never
a necessary accompaniment
to directness.

Don't allow others to invalidate
your sense of humour just because
you
don't enjoy laughing 28
at someone else's expense.

29 Responding with
'I don't mind'
whenever you are asked
to make a choice
reinforces the habit
of putting your responsibility
in the hands of others.

It is easy to hide our need to be liked
behind the pronouncement
of needing to care **30**
for others.

——————— July ———————

31

If your intuition tells you
you cannot trust
a person or situation,
that is your reality
and no amount
of rationalising or
wishful thinking
will make it otherwise.

1 It helps to give vent, out loud,
to all the unforgivable and awful
things you've wanted to say
to someone
– while you're alone!
Then you will be able to distinguish
rubbish from reality.

You don't have to take a joke
if you didn't ask for it. 2

3 Continuing to talk to someone
while they are watching TV
or on the telephone
gives a clear message
that what you have to say
is not important
and not worth listening to.

The most likely way
you'll get what you want
is to ask for it
directly and specifically. 4

5 It is essential,
while remaining true to oneself,
to acknowledge others'
different and separate realities
– otherwise we can get stuck in
self-righteous delusion.

It is possible
to be criticised and
feel loved
at the same time. 6

7 We reject
real-life opportunities
to be nurtured
by waiting
for a magical caretaker
to materialise and
meet all our fantasy requirements.

Trust your gut response
— it is always a sign that
you need to think twice 8
about something before
opening your mouth.

——————— August ———————

9 The prospect of
no longer filling one's time
with caring duties to others,
lovingly fulfilled, is the prospect of
a huge and terrifying
void.

Our sexuality doesn't cease to exist
when others
cease to see us
as sexual objects. 10

11 When your reason
for not
being honest with someone
is that the truth
would be hurtful, remember that
your own fear of rejection
can also hold you back.

Instead of stopping at:
'You're great', or 'You're amazing',
try making the extra effort
to express specifically what
you appreciate in someone. **12**

13
Short-term compromises
have the habit of becoming
long-term prisons.

If someone says no to you,
they are probably saying no
– not rejecting you outright. # 14

15 It is possible to enjoy the
havoc of your hormones
if you can let go of
your need
to be in total control of everything.

As soon as you feel contempt
for someone,
you place yourself
above them. **16**

17 If you find
you are sexually unaroused,
this doesn't imply
you are a sexual failure
– more likely, the conditions you need
to feel sexual arousal are not being met.

There is a curious arrogance in
assuming *others* have the right to rest
while insisting that we,
ourselves, can go on
forever. **18**

19

Our perceptions
are distorted
when our feelings run high.

When offering someone a criticism,
keep to one item of behaviour only.
That is all
anyone can listen to
or take in
at any one time.

20

21

If you don't feel
like smiling,
don't smile.

We put so much emotional energy
into finding and keeping
the Perfect Relationship
that we often miss out on
the more enduring joys
of friendship.

22

August

23 Enjoy your emotions
— those who criticise you
for expressing them
have usually lost touch
with their own.

If you find yourself insisting that
someone should follow
your advice,
you're probably
bullying them. 24

25

You may not be able
to have it all
— but you can have it
both ways!

It is low self-esteem
which encourages us
to suffer pain in silence
rather than
suffer
possible
disapproval. # 26

27

People change
at their own pace
— we can't accelerate
the process to suit our own needs.

Treasure those whose company prompts
you to be playful and have fun
— their gift to you is
priceless.

28

29 As soon as you start
worrying about
the judgement of others,
you cease being creative.

Learn to distinguish between
straining and stretching yourself
– the former leads to injury,
the latter
to development. 30

31

Even the role of the 'carer'
can be addictive.

1 Next time you catch sight of
yourself in the mirror,
blow yourself a little kiss
— before the self-criticism starts!

It's easier to demand something
from the standpoint of reproach
than to ask openly and risk
exposure and
vulnerability. **2**

3 Feeling sorry for someone
has nothing to do with equality
– it involves one person
feeling kindly, benevolent
and usually superior to
another.

It is harder to confront
a sexist or racist comment
from someone we care for
than from someone
we are quite happy to dismiss. 4

5 It is a lifelong challenge,
  as women, to become
  subjects
of our bodies when we have
only experienced them as
objects
in the eyes of others.

When you offer someone a criticism,
  try and offer it as a gift
    rather than
  a punishment. 6

7 A deep inner emptiness is
the abiding experience
of most women
– the biggest cream cake,
the hottest sex,
the most fulfilling occupation,
the most adoring partner
will do no more than assuage
that emptiness for a while.

You can allow others to have feelings
without taking on
the responsibility
for having caused them. 8

9

Blaming ourselves too readily
protects us from the insecurity
of accepting that life,
by its very nature,
is unpredictable and imperfect.

If you want help with a difficulty,
remember that whining
and whinging
make most people go
instantly deaf!

10

11

Our own self put-downs
are often far more cruel
than those we hear
from other people.

Beat the hell
out of a large cushion
before trying to talk clearly
to someone you're angry with.

12

September

13 Wanting to say no
without ever feeling guilty
is like wanting to climb
a challenging mountain
without ever feeling tired.

Don't expect support
– just be open to it. **14**

15

Seeking revenge
is often understandable
– but always aggressive.

If you're shopping
to combat neediness and depression,
you can limit yourself to
looking and longing
by leaving your credit cards
at home. **16**

17

Even if you take a risk
and make a mess
of the situation,
there is always something positive
you can learn from the experience.

Emotions don't have to be
either one thing or the other.
They are usually a mixture of both.

18

19 Who am I
when I am
not attending to,
thinking of,
caring for others?
– *that* is the question.

Making a clear choice
to put another's needs first is different
from self-sacrifice
on the altar of 20
your own masochism.

21 Holding on to
your own truth
is a constant but
necessary challenge
in a world
which encourages and rewards lies.

Next time you hear yourself saying,
'I don't mind',
take a moment to check
you are being honest
with yourself. **22**

23 If you unexpectedly find yourself with time on your hands, instead of filling it by doing something useful, try passing the time just *being*.

We trade in the currency of guilt so automatically that we are hardly aware of it until we count our emotional pennies and seek to balance the accounts. 24

25

If you want your
criticism to be heard,
you will have a better chance
if you confine yourself
to criticising
one single aspect
of the person's behaviour.

It is very hard to rid ourselves
of the conviction that if only
we could get it right,
things would be different.

26

27

Manipulating someone 'for their own good' is a misappropriation of power — and such efforts are usually resisted.

You cannot
feel sorry for yourself
and skip
at the same time.

28

29

Never confuse
a self put-down
with real humility.

If you are depressed, tired or ill,
it is folly to try and
force yourself
into a state of sexual arousal.

30

1 Telling someone
they've no right to be angry
will only fuel the flames.

If you feel offended,
say so
– without causing offence
in return. 2

3 Offer a compliment as a gift
— freely given
without regard to
the other person's
adequate response.

Your feelings are simply your feelings
— seeking someone to blame
for causing them 4
won't help them disappear.

5 When you preface
your statement with:
'This may sound silly, but …',
'I know this isn't important, but … ',
'Of course, I'm no expert, but … ',
you discourage listeners
from taking you seriously.

Remember you can (and do)
survive being told:
'No.'
– and so can others. 6

7 Next time you find yourself
gossiping about a friend,
ask yourself
if there is something
you have avoided saying directly to them.

Have a temper tantrum occasionally
– just don't try and
communicate clearly
at the same time. 8

9 It is worth building up
a resource of particular
activities, people or places
which you know
will restore you when
you experience the
inevitable rejections of life.

Take time to concentrate
on the process and pleasure of eating
instead of
hastily munching 10
on the run.

11

Our need to be liked
seduces us away from the path
to real personal power.

Even if you're embarrassed
or they're embarrassed,
it is still worth saying
thank you.

12

13 Self-esteem
is buying something
which fits comfortably
and truthfully
instead of squeezing into a smaller size
and playing a self-punishing game of
make-believe.

If you are becoming a little too earnest
in your solicitude towards another,
consider whether you are
giving precisely what you
would like to receive yourself. **14**

15 Each time
we swallow back
our emotions,
we deny a vital part of our experience.

Being assertive does not mean
always getting what you want:
this could only be achieved by
overriding others'
feelings and needs **16**
along the way.

17

If someone is in tears,
being with them
silently and peacefully
is often more helpful
than rushing around
for cups of tea or tissues.

If there's a stone in your shoe,
you can remove it
– or continue to walk,
hoping the pain will
eventually go away.

18

19 Next time you find yourself
travelling
on the merry-go-round
of self-sacrifice,
ask yourself,
'Is there really nothing I want in return
… ever?'

It is quite a challenge
to leave an argument
with a clear statement of difference
rather than insisting that one of you
has to be right
and the other **20**
wrong.

21

Instead of being consumed
with envious feelings
towards others,
take a moment to consider whether
there are some different choices you
could be making in your own life.

You *can* probably please everybody
all of the time
– but is it really
worth the cost? 22

23 Don't wait until
the next time it happens
before you say something
— making the time to confront
the situation before it re-occurs
increases your chances
of handling it effectively.

The power that will be released
when women stop punishing themselves
will be
an enormous force **24**
for change in the world.

25

Practise walking lightly through heavy situations.

Far from being grounds for criticism, the quality of over-sensitivity should be celebrated as a beacon in an emotionally unenlightened and deadened world.

26

27 Blaming others
is the easiest way
to divert ourselves
from taking responsibility
for our own feelings
and behaviour.

Excessive criticism
will severely damage
anyone's sense of self-worth. 28

29 The role of 'carer'
wraps us
like a familiar warm coat
— we are afraid that, without it,
we might freeze to death.

Whether making love or a fruit cake
try focusing
on the pleasure of the process
rather than worrying about
the quality of the end product. 30

31 Even if you keep her
well-hidden
most of the time,
allow the witch in you
some clear means of expression
every now and then.

——————— November ———————

1 What are you really waiting for?

Acting a little crazily
(in the eyes of others)
is often the best way
to retain your sanity. 2

3 Don't confuse
blaming and punishing yourself
with genuinely taking
responsibility
for your behaviour.

Other people's feelings
do not necessarily
have anything to do with
your behaviour.
4

5 Gossip can be like a drug
— easily available,
slightly taboo,
temporarily enjoyable
but ultimately
poisonous to the entire system.

The energy wasted in worrying
whether someone is hurt or
angry or disappointed in you,
could be saved by
a simple, clear, direct enquiry
to the person concerned. 6

7 There is no single
right
way.

Contrary to popular belief,
anger can be a highly
constructive emotion. 8

9 Never be ashamed
to be 'heart-full'
– even if you're in
heartless surroundings.

For most of us,
rising to the challenge of being
noble and selfless in the midst
of others' demands,
requires less personal effort
than facing the possibility of
rejection. **10**

11

Failing to confront
unfair criticism
is an effective way of
putting yourself down.

Saying no to someone one cares for is,
for most women,
as natural as cutting off
one's arm.

12

13

A hairline crack
in a relationship easily grows
into an unbridgeable chasm.

Know when to remove yourself
silently
from a situation
in which you feel uneasy.

14

15 When someone knows
clearly and specifically
what you would like to be
different,
they find it easier to hear and accept
what is currently
unsatisfactory.

The unfortunate fact about tiredness
is that at the very moment
we most need to stop,
we are least able to
climb down from the
masochistic treadmill. **16**

November

17 There are many
erotic pleasures
to be enjoyed
in everyday life, if we don't confuse
them with sexual activity.

Next time you're swamped with guilt,
ask yourself
what you're angry
about. 18

19 Authority becomes oppression when we don't allow others to express their responses to our actions and decisions.

20 Exercising your right to choose may well incur reproach, because being reminded of one's own ability to choose is often an uncomfortable experience.

21 Instead of politely waiting
to interrupt someone
who is abusing you
over the phone,
you can hang up.

The more anxious I am
about being rejected,
the more I will
tend to imagine that I am. 22

23

Giving up the need to be seen to be right allows for a lot more flexibility in life.

Don't wait until someone is leaving or dying before you tell them how much you value them.

24

25 When your heart melts,
don't be afraid
to let it show.

Often we feel empowered
to criticise someone
only when we feel the
unassailable authority of being *right*
— but any criticism given from this
superior standpoint
will always be met
with a defensive response. 26

27 Clear anger is a
vital
though unfamiliar aspect of
love.

28 Singing – or simply allowing your voice
to make large sounds
– is a wonderful
release of tension.

29

However subtly
you convey aggression
in your manner,
it will inevitably trigger
an aggressive response
in the other person,
even if it is not openly expressed.

The best way to stop feeling threatened
by someone expressing their anger is
to become more familiar
and comfortable
with this emotion
in yourself.

30

1 The intention to set aside
30 minutes a day for oneself is easy.
Achieving this aim,
for most of us,
is the equivalent of climbing
an emotional Everest.

Laugh when you want to laugh
– not just to be one of the crowd. 2

3 There is nothing
so personally empowering
as making a clear choice.

Sometimes it is wiser 4
to keep quiet.

5 It is more honest
to use the word 'angry'
to describe your feelings
when this is appropriate,
rather than settling for 'upset' or 'hurt'.

Never attempt to offer a criticism
of your lover
when you are in bed together.
Make a time to talk
when you are both less naked. 6

7
Focus on *one* thing
you would like to be different
in any given situation
– this is the first vital step
out of the mire of helplessness.

Are you only holding back because
you can't guarantee
getting it
right? 8

9 Rubbing someone's face
in their own inadequacies
offers us temporary relief
from punishing the weak and
imperfect aspects of ourselves.

If you exercise your right
to change your mind, remember
the accompanying responsibility
— to communicate
your decision
as soon as possible. 10

11 It is easier to accuse resentfully
than risk
making a small request
directly.

Listen to and trust
what your heart tells you. **12**

13

Don't sabotage yourself
by tackling a situation
that is too difficult to handle
– this only leads to
loss of confidence
and despair.

The torment of punishing ourselves
for not getting it right
is often preferable
to experiencing the helplessness
of piloting
uncertainly
through chaos. # 14

15 When dealing with money, we often allow ourselves to be manipulated by our own fears and a low sense of self-worth.

Starting from a place of self-acceptance enables us to be intimate without swamping others or being swamped ourselves. **16**

17 If you feel manipulated by another's question or statement, encourage them to express their feelings or wishes *directly* to you.

18 Our self-esteem is strengthened when we stop imposing grandiose and impossible expectations on ourselves.

19

Fear of looking foolish
prevents us criticising
someone directly
because, in doing so,
we risk finding out
that our perceptions are
wrong.

Through clearly expressing
our anger,
we are able to touch
the edge
of our joy.

20

21 We tend to overestimate
the number of people
who are truly dependent on us
for their survival.

The greater the loss of
my self-esteem,
the more I depend on
others' approval
to compensate for that loss. 22

23 It is the *being* of sexuality
which we have lost
through our obsession
with the *doing*.

24 If someone criticises you unjustly,
it is important to
express your disagreement
but also invite the other person
to clarify
what has prompted
the criticism.

25

A simple heartfelt
appreciative comment
is the best gift of all.

It is easier to package a request
using reproach and guilt
as leverage
than risk being told
no. **26**

27

Treat yourself with
gentleness and kindness.
It may sound simple,
but is often the hardest thing to do.

Short-term indulgence in self-pity
doesn't do anyone any harm
– in the longer term, self-pity becomes
a ball and chain
on our expression of
personal power.

28

29 Don't confine sexuality
to the genitals
— sexual energy spreads
throughout our bodies
and throughout our lives.

We spend so much time
anticipating and reacting to others
that it is easy
to lose sight of
our own feelings and needs. **30**

31 Whatever you choose
to give,
make sure it is duty free.

A Book of Your Own is typeset in
12/14pt Monotype Perpetua,
designed by Eric Gill in 1925.
It was originally commissioned by
Beatrice Warde and Stanley Morison
at the Monotype type foundry,
Great Britain.

This book was designed by
Stephen Parker at Namara Design.